★ THE NEXT GOAT

CHLOE KIM

CORINA JEFFRIES

PowerKiDS press

Published in 2025 by The Rosen Publishing Group, Inc.
2544 Clinton Street, Buffalo, NY 14224

First Edition

Editor: Greg Roza
Book Design: Rachel Rising

Photo Credits: Cover, PCN Photography/Alamy Stock Photo; Cover, pp. 1, 3, 4, 6, 8, 10, 12, 14, 16, 18, 20, 22, 23, 24 Pixacon/Shutterstock.com; Cover Farhanz9/Shutterstock.com; Cover, p. 1 Alhovik/Shutterstock.com; p. 4 mitry Naumov/Shutterstock.com; p. 5 Kathy Hutchins/Shutterstock.com; p. 7 Pascal Vosicki/Shutterstock.com; p. 8 Muhammad Ahsan Ashfaq/Shutterstock.com; p. 9 Aflo Co. Ltd./Alamy Stock Photo; p. 11 Action Plus Sports Images/Alamy Stock Photo; p. 12 STILLFX/Shutterstock.com; p. 13 NTB/Alamy Stock Photo; p. 15 Leonard Zhukovsky/Shutterstock.com; p.16 https://commons.wikimedia.org/wiki/File:Snowboarding_pictogram.svg; p. 17 NurPhoto SRL/Alamy Stock Photo; p. 18 Exhibex/Shutterstock.com; p. 19 Tinseltown/Shutterstock.com; p. 20 dyoma/Shutterstock.com; p. 21 Featureflash Photo Agency/Shutterstock.com.

Library of Congress Cataloging-in-Publication Data

Names: Jeffries, Corina, author.
Title: Chloe Kim / Corina Jeffries.
Description: Buffalo, NY : PowerKids Press, [2025] | Series: The next goat | Includes index.
Identifiers: LCCN 2024031014 (print) | LCCN 2024031015 (ebook) | ISBN 9781499449648 (library binding) | ISBN 9781499449631 (paperback) | ISBN 9781499449655 (ebook)
Subjects: LCSH: Kim, Chloe 2000–Juvenile literature. | Women Olympic athletes–United States–Biography–Juvenile literature. | Snowboarders–United States–Biography–Juvenile literature. | Asian American athletes–United States–Biography–Juvenile literature. | Women Olympic athletes–United States–Biography–Juvenile literature.
Classification: LCC GV857.S57 J43 2025 (print) | LCC GV857.S57 (ebook) | DDC 796.939092 [B]–dc23/eng/20240705
LC record available at https://lccn.loc.gov/2024031014
LC ebook record available at https://lccn.loc.gov/2024031015

Manufactured in the United States of America

CPSIA Compliance Information: Batch #CWPK25. For Further Information contact Rosen Publishing at 1-800-237-9932.

CONTENTS

MEET CHLOE!

Chloe Kim is a snowboarder and up-and-comer in the world of sports. Some think she's the next greatest of all time!

In 2018, at the Winter Olympics in Pyeongchang, South Korea, Kim became the youngest woman to come in first place in the women's **half-pipe**. She was just 17 years old! By the time she was 22, Kim was already a two-time Olympic gold **medalist**. She's also won big at ESPN's X Games. Read on to find out even more about Chloe Kim.

This is a photograph of Kim after winning her second Olympic gold medal at the 2022 Winter Games in Beijing, China.

GROWING UP

Chloe Kim was born on April 23, 2000. She grew up in southern California, with her father, mother, and two older sisters. Chloe's parents are originally from South Korea. Her father, Jong Jin Kim, took her to a nearby mountain in California when she was just four. That's where she got her start! She began **competing** when she was just six.

When Chloe was eight she traveled to Geneva, Switzerland, where she stayed with her aunt. She won a youth snowboard competition while there!

WHAT THEY'RE SAYING

Chloe said this about her father and learning to snowboard: "We learned how to snowboard together. We both had no idea what we were doing."

Geneva, Switzerland, is in Europe. It's on one end of Lake Geneva. The area is surrounded by the Jura Mountains.

X GAMES STAR

When she was 13, Kim joined the U.S. Snowboarding Team. Although she was still too young to compete in the Olympics, Kim wowed fans at the 2014 X Games in Aspen, Colorado. She won a silver medal in the **superpipe** competition, making her the youngest person to win an X Games medal at the time.

When she was 14, Kim competed in the 2015 X Games in Aspen and Oslo, Norway. She became the youngest gold medalist in X Games history at the time!

WINTER GAMES

Kim makes snowboarding look easy at the 2014 X Games.

Kim's X Games success continued in 2016. That year she became the youngest person to win two gold medals at an X Games competition.

That same year, Kim competed at the U.S. Snowboarding Grand Prix (a yearly competition that decides who will make the U.S. Olympic Team for half-pipe). She became the first woman to land back-to-back **1080** spins at a snowboarding competition. She scored a perfect 100 points! The only other **athlete** to accomplish that feat is the great Shaun White.

WHAT THEY'RE SAYING

"Her dad and mum were never in a hurry to push her into events, but she has kept progressing and moving up and up to bigger events. She's moving faster than I had even thought possible."

—Kim's first snowboard coach Ben Wiser

Kim flies high during her gold-winning run at the 2016 X Games in Oslo, Norway.

2016 WINTER YOUTH OLYMPICS

Thanks to her amazing display of skill at the X Games and the Grand Prix, Kim earned a trip to the 2016 Winter Youth Olympics in Lillehammer, Norway. Team USA chose Kim to carry the American flag for the opening parade.

Kim set a few records! She became the first woman to earn a gold medal in snowboarding at the Youth Winter Olympics. She also received the highest snowboarding score in the history of the Youth Olympic Games. Kim also won a gold medal in the **slopestyle** event.

Kim (middle) poses with the second- and third-place winners at the 2016 Youth Winter Olympics.

2018 WINTER OLYMPICS

Kim's first Winter Olympic Games was another great success. It was extra sweet because it was in South Korea. She has many fans there.

Only 17 years old, Kim became the youngest woman in history to win an Olympic gold medal in snowboarding. She became the first woman to land back-to-back 1080s at the Olympics. That was only after she had already **clinched** the gold medal! Later, U.S. snowboarding coach Rick Bower said it was the "best run that she's ever done."

WHAT THEY'RE SAYING

"She's pushing the boundaries of what's possible for women's snowboarding. She's doing tricks that some of the men don't even want to. It's pretty crazy. She is the greatest women's snowboarder of all time, by far."

—Arielle Gold, snowboarder, bronze medalist at the 2018 Winter Olympics

Kim celebrates after winning a gold medal at the 2018 Winter Olympics.

2022 WINTER OLYMPICS

The 2022 Winter Olympics were held in Beijing, China. Kim was prepared to amaze the crowd once again. For her first run, Kim received a score of 94, making her the leader. No other female snowboarders were able to beat this score!

Still, Kim continued to push herself. She wanted to take her performance to a new level. For her next two runs, Kim attempted to land a 1260—three and a half spins. However, she failed to land it.

Kim's win at the 2022 Winter Olympics set another record. Kim became the first woman to win a gold medal in back-to-back Winter Olympics for the half-pipe.

RISING STAR

Besides snowboarding, Kim is a busy person! She has attended Princeton University, and can speak three languages (English, Korean, and French). Kim's popularity on the half-pipe has gained her several roles on television and in movies. She appeared in the 2019 movie *Charlie's Angels*, and in an episode of the cartoon *Scooby-Doo and Guess Who?* She was also on *The Masked Singer.*

Kim even has a Barbie doll made in her likeness! It comes with a snowboard, cold-weather outfit, and a gold medal.

PRINCETON UNIVERSITY

In March 2022, Kim's likeness was used to develop a character for the popular video game *Fortnite*.

WHAT'S NEXT?

Kim has had to deal with racism. This was hard for her for a long time. During the 2018 ESPY Awards, Kim won the Best Female Athlete of the Year Award, and she used her acceptance speech to speak out against racism.

With so many awards and honors at such a young age, some sports fans wonder if Chloe Kim is already the GOAT of snowboarding!

WHAT THEY'RE SAYING

"I think, every time I'm on the mountain, I'm just so thankful to be there."
—Chloe Kim

Kim won three ESPY Awards in 2018: Best Female Athlete, Best Female Olympian, and Best Female Action Sport Athlete.

GLOSSARY

athlete: A person who is trained in or good at games and exercises that require physical skill, endurance, and strength.

clinch: To assure winning something.

compete: To strive for something (as a prize or reward) for which others are also striving.

half-pipe: A U-shaped, high-sided ramp used especially in snowboarding, skateboarding, or in-line skating.

medalist: Someone who wins first, second, or third place in a sporting event where the awards are gold, silver, and bronze medals (awards).

superpipe: A larger version of a half-pipe used in winter sports.

slopestyle: A snowboarding or skiing event in which participants perform tricks and jumps on a course with multiple slopes, ramps, and rails.

1080: A trick where the snowboarder jumps and makes three full rotations, or spins, before landing.

FOR MORE INFORMATION

BOOKS

Goldstein, Margaret J. *Meet Chloe Kim: Snowboarding Superstar*. Minneapolis, MN: Lerner Publishing Group, 2023.

Golkar, Golriz. *Chloe Kim*. Minneapolis, MN: Bellwether Media, 2024.

Streetor, Anthony. *Winter Olympics All-Time Greats*. Mendota Heights, MN: Press Box Books, 2024.

WEBSITES

Team USA: Chloe Kim
www.teamusa.com/profiles/chloe-kim
Read more about Chloe Kim and see videos of her winning gold medals in the Olympics.

U.S. Ski and Snowboard Foundation
usskiandsnowboard.org
Visit this website to learn more about 10 winter sports, including snowboarding, that are funded by the U.S. Ski and Snowboard Foundation.

INDEX